10+

Earth's
Shifting Surface

Robert Snedden

Chicago, Illinois

www.heinemannraintree.com
Visit our website to find out
more information about
Heinemann-Raintree books.

To order:

☎ Phone 888-454-2279
💻 Visit www.heinemannraintree.com
to browse our catalog and order online.

Edited by James Nixon
Page layout by sprout.uk.com limited
Original illustrations © Discovery Books Limited 2009
Illustrated by sprout.uk.com limited
Picture research by James Nixon
Originated by Discovery Books Limited
Printed and bound by CTPS (China Translation and
    Printing Services Ltd)

14 13 12 11 10
10 9 8 7 6 5 4 3 2 1

Library of Congress Cataloging-in-Publication Data
Snedden, Robert.
    Earth's shifting surface / Robert Snedden.
        p. cm. -- (Sci-hi. Earth and space science)
    Includes bibliographical references and index.
    ISBN 978-1-4109-3349-2 (hc) -- ISBN 978-1-4109-
3359-1 (pb) 1. Plate tectonics--Juvenile literature. 2.
Earth--Surface--Juvenile literature. 3. Geodynamics--
Juvenile literature. I. Title.
    QE511.4.S59 2008
    551.1'36--dc22
                                2009003532

Acknowledgments
We would like to thank the following for permission
to reproduce photographs: Alamy: cover inset (Kevin
Schafer/Peter Arnold Inc.); p. 38 (Mike Goldwater);
Alfred Wegener Institute: pp. 14 top, 15 bottom;
Corbis: pp. 7 bottom (Raymond Gehman), 14 (Louie
Psihoyos), 36 (Bettmann); Getty Images: pp. 20
(Sigurgeir Jonasson/Nordic Photos), 23 top (Thomas
J. Abercrombie/National Geographic), 32 top (Toru
Yamanaka), 32 bottom (Toru Yamanaka), 33 (Majid);
Istockphoto.com: pp. 23 top (James Steidl), 25 (David
Ciemny), 27 (Valentina Petrova); NASA: p. 40 bottom;
Nevada Seismological Laboratory: p. 11 top; Annabel
Savery: p. 24; Science Photo Library: pp. 6 (Lynette
Cook), 7 top (Joe Tucciarone), 9 (W. Habby, Lamont-
Doherty Earth Observatory), 41 (NASA); Shutterstock:
pp. 4, 5 (Julien Grondin), 11 bottom (Andreas Danti),
21 (Bjartue Snorrason), 29 top, 29 bottom (A. S.
Zain), 34; U.S. Geological Society: cover & pp. 30 (R. E.
Wallace), 31 top (W. C. Mendenhall), 31 bottom (H. G.
Wilshire), 36 bottom, 37 middle, 37 top (D. R. Crandell),
37 bottom, 40 top; Wikipedia: p. 15 top.

Cover photograph of Mount St. Helens, Washington
state, reproduced with permission of U.S. Geological
Society.

We would like to thank content consultant Suzy
Gazlay and text consultant Nancy Harris for their
invaluable help in the preparation of this book.

Contents

Why are these sea cliffs rising over 1 cm (0.4 in) each year? Find out on page 13!

How are giant waves caused by tremors in Earth? Find out on page 29!

Some words are shown in bold, **like this**. These words are explained in the glossary. You will find important information and definitions underlined, <u>like this</u>.

THE ACTIVE EARTH

Did you know that the planet on which we live is always on the move? You probably know that Earth spins through space around the Sun. But did you realize that the surface beneath your feet is constantly shifting, too? The ground is not as solid as it seems.

THE SHIFTING LAND

When you look at a landscape it seems to be unchanging. But what we see is just a moment in Earth's long history. Millions of years ago, the land you look at would have been very different. Millions of years from now, it will be different again.

Broken surface

The surface of Earth, or **crust**, is not a single, unbroken sheet of rock. Like the cracked shell of an egg, it is formed from a number of giant pieces. These pieces are called **tectonic plates**. They float on top of **molten** (liquid) rock beneath them. <u>Slow **currents** (movements) in the molten rock keep the massive plates moving slowly but constantly.</u>

An erupting volcano is a sign that there are tectonic plates on the move. The energy of the plates melt rock deep underground. This molten rock may then erupt suddenly onto the surface.

Plate power

The effects of plate movements can be sudden and devastating. The moving plates can open up volcanoes and set off catastrophic earthquakes. The shifting plates also bring about changes over long periods of time. Where one plate collides with another, huge mountain ranges can be slowly pushed up. This process can last millions of years.

Planet Earth

Around 4.5 billion years ago, the Sun formed from a giant cloud of dust in space. From the remnants of that dust cloud, the Sun's family of planets took shape. Some, such as Saturn and Jupiter, are giant gas planets. Others, such as Mars and our own planet Earth, are rocky worlds.

Ancient rocks

Early Earth was uninviting. Its bubbling, **molten** surface was under constant attack by **meteorites** that rained in from space. Slowly the surface of the planet cooled. The oldest rocks found on Earth are around 3.8 billion years old. By this time, Earth's surface had become solid. Just how Earth changed from a planet of molten material to one with a hard **crust** made of slow-moving **tectonic plates** remains a mystery.

After the planets formed, there was a lot of material left over. Much of this rained down on Earth's surface. This destructive meteor bombardment may have lasted millions of years.

COSMIC COLLISION

Scientists have a **theory** (idea) that Earth was almost destroyed shortly after it formed. A massive object as big as the planet Mars collided with it. The Moon was formed from the debris that was knocked off Earth. The surface of the planet that remained was turned molten by the force of the collision.

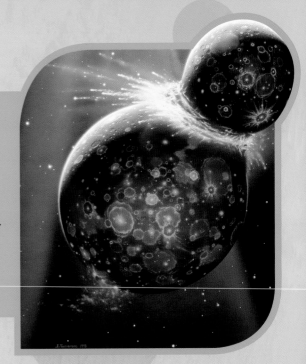

Continents

The vast, rocky continents are believed to have been formed as the crust cooled. Lighter materials rose up to "float" on the denser material below. Volcanic eruptions added to this top layer of material. As the **continents** grew in size, the rocks in the middle moved far away from volcanic activity at the plate edges. As a result they have survived for millions of years. These ancient rock formations are called **shields**. Today the continents are built around these old rocks.

Part of the Canadian Shield in Alberta, Canada. This is the ancient heart of the North American continent.

Earth's crust

The crust is Earth's outer skin. It is the part we know best, because we live on it. It is a very small part of the whole planet. In terms of thickness, the crust is like a postage stamp stuck to a soccer ball.

As young planet Earth cooled down over millions of years, the inside of the planet began to separate out into different layers. The rocky crust formed on the surface of the world, like the skin that forms on a glass of warm milk as it cools.

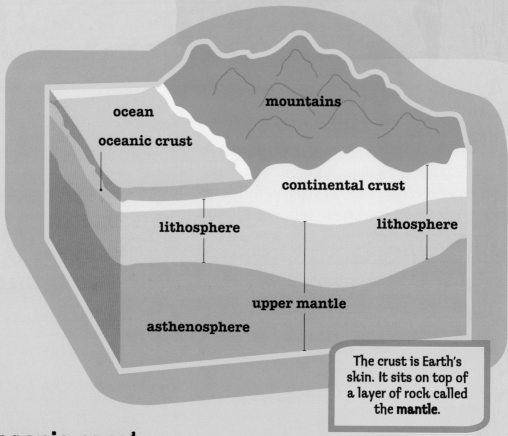

ocean

oceanic crust

mountains

continental crust

lithosphere

lithosphere

upper mantle

asthenosphere

> The crust is Earth's skin. It sits on top of a layer of rock called the **mantle**.

Oceanic crust

The **oceanic crust** is made up of younger rock than the **continental crust**. No oceanic crust older than 220 million years has yet been found. It is also thinner than the **continental crust**, about 6 to 10 km (4 to 6 miles) thick on average.

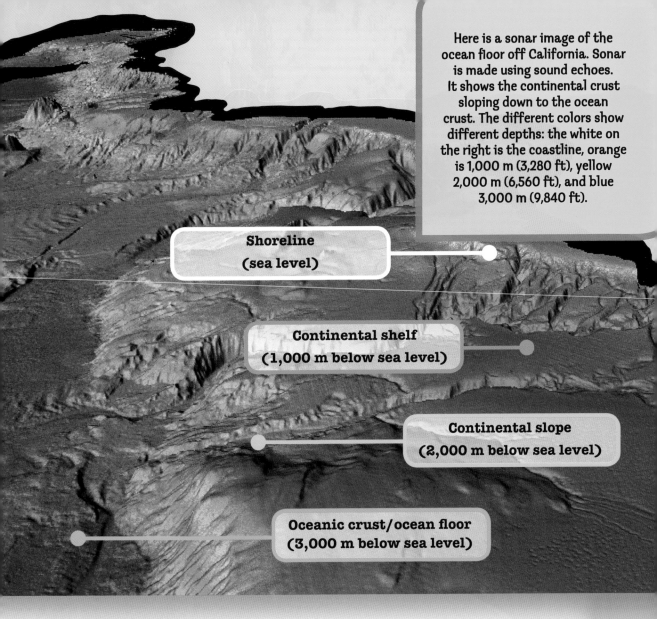

Here is a sonar image of the ocean floor off California. Sonar is made using sound echoes. It shows the continental crust sloping down to the ocean crust. The different colors show different depths: the white on the right is the coastline, orange is 1,000 m (3,280 ft), yellow 2,000 m (6,560 ft), and blue 3,000 m (9,840 ft).

Shoreline
(sea level)

Continental shelf
(1,000 m below sea level)

Continental slope
(2,000 m below sea level)

Oceanic crust/ocean floor
(3,000 m below sea level)

Continental crust

As the name suggests, this is the type of crust that forms the continents.

The continental crust is the oldest and thickest part of the crust. It reaches down between 30 and 70 km (20 and 45 miles) below the surface. It is at its deepest underneath mountain ranges. The oldest rocks (shields) of the continental crust are over 3 billion years old. The continental crust doesn't stop at the ocean's edge. It continues for a short distance beneath the water as the **continental shelf**. The continental slope leads it down to the deep ocean floor.

Inside Earth

No one has ever seen what the inside of Earth looks like. The deepest mine shafts ever dug only go down around 4 km (2.5 miles) and it is 6,150 km (3,565 miles) to the center of Earth. Yet scientists know what Earth is made from.

Earth's layers

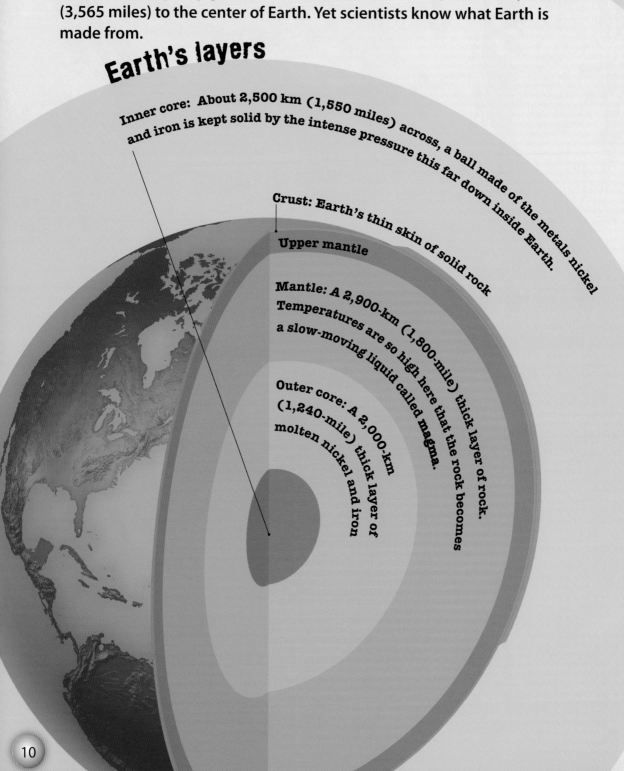

Inner core: About 2,500 km (1,550 miles) across, a ball made of the metals nickel and iron is kept solid by the intense pressure this far down inside Earth.

Crust: Earth's thin skin of solid rock

Upper mantle

Mantle: A 2,900-km (1,800-mile) thick layer of rock. Temperatures are so high here that the rock becomes a slow-moving liquid called magma.

Outer core: A 2,000-km (1,240-mile) thick layer of molten nickel and iron

SET THE PLANET RINGING

How do scientists know what the inside of Earth is like? They analyze **shock waves**. Try it yourself. Get a drinking glass and tap it gently with your fingernail. Listen to the sound it makes. Now fill the glass with water and tap it again. Can you hear the difference in the sound? Even with your eyes closed, you could tell whether the glass was full or empty just by tapping it.

Revealing waves

Think of the effect of an earthquake as being like a giant bump that sets Earth ringing. The earthquake sends shock waves through the planet. As these waves encounter different materials, they change speed and direction. They may be stopped altogether.

Some waves travel through both solids and liquids. Others only travel through solids. By using **seismometers** to measure the way these waves travel through Earth, scientists have been able to build up a picture of the inside of Earth.

Scientists use seismometers to measure shock waves caused by earthquakes.

seismometer

seismometer reading

Shock waves

Floating plates

Each tectonic plate is made from a solid slab of lithosphere—a combination of the crust plus the uppermost part of the mantle. Immediately below the **lithosphere** is another layer, called the **asthenosphere**. It is this partly-melted layer of the mantle that the plates move on.

Upsetting the balance

The massive plates floating on the mantle find a balance. The balance can be upset after an ice age. When thick ice sheets form over the land, their massive weight pushes the crust lower down into the mantle. As the ice melts, the crust slowly rebounds and rises up again.

Parts of Scandinavia in northern Europe are rising at a rate of about 1 cm (0.4 in) a year. This is still happening even though most of the ice disappeared more than 10,000 years ago. To restore the balance, the crust still has to rise a further 200 m (660 ft).

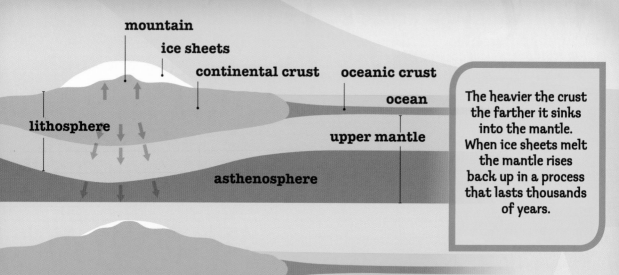

mountain

ice sheets

continental crust   oceanic crust

ocean

lithosphere

upper mantle

asthenosphere

The heavier the crust the farther it sinks into the mantle. When ice sheets melt the mantle rises back up in a process that lasts thousands of years.

The mantle slowly rises as the ice melts.

The mantle's rebound is complete.

The coastline around Hudson Bay in Canada was pressed down to sea level during the last ice age. When the ice sheets melted, the land sprang back up. The sea cliffs around the bay are now hundreds of meters high.

Carrying continents

Most plates have continents on them. A continent is really a huge mass of lighter rocks sitting on top of a plate. As the plates move, the continents are carried with them. The thicker continental crust sinks farther down into the mantle than the oceanic crust. This is just like a ship full of cargo will ride lower in the water than the same ship when it is empty.

TRY THIS

A Rebound Model

Fill a container big enough to float a wooden block with water. The block represents the crust. Pile ice cubes on the block to recreate an ice age. Note how the block sinks lower in the water. Let the ice melt and see how the block rises back up.

Alfred Wegener's BIG IDEA

Alfred Wegener (1880–1930) was the first person to figure out that the **continents** are moving on gigantic sliding **tectonic plates**. He suggested that 250 million years ago the continents were gathered together in one giant mass.

Wegener found **fossils** from identical types of plants and animals on both sides of the Atlantic Ocean. Wegener believed that this was evidence that South America and Africa must have been joined together in the past.

Fossil hunters have discovered fossils from the same kinds of dinosaurs on either side of the Atlantic Ocean. It is a clue that the continents were once joined.

Gathering clues

* As early as the 16th century, mapmakers had noticed how closely the coasts of Africa and South America seemed to fit to each other.

* In the early 19th century, it was discovered that the rocks of Brazil in South America were similar to those of the Congo in West Africa.

* **Naturalists** studying the wildlife of both continents discovered identical types of snakes and lizards in South America and in Africa.

Scientists at the beginning of the 20th century wrongly believed that the continents were once joined by bridges of land.

Land bridges

Wegener put forward his **theory** of continental drift in 1912 to explain how the continents had moved apart. He was mocked by most people. Many scientists of the time believed that the continents had been joined by bridges of land. They felt these bridges had long since vanished beneath the ocean.

An idea before its time

Wegener didn't live to see his ideas accepted. He died on an expedition in Greenland shortly after his fiftieth birthday in 1930. It wasn't until the 1950s, when scientists began to discover the Atlantic Ocean was widening, that Wegener's ideas began to find favor. We will look at that discovery later.

Wegener was buried in Greenland where he died on an expedition. He got lost in a blizzard. His body was found six months later by his brother Kurt. The grave is marked by a cross made out of drilling tools.

"Das Große Eis"
Aufnahme: Dr. Georgi

The Drifting Continents

Wegener's theory is now widely accepted. Around 250 million years ago, all of Earth's **landmass** was gathered together in one place—the supercontinent Pangaea. Scientists believe that the **continents** have since slowly drifted to their present-day locations. In perhaps another 250 million years, the continents will be back together again in the new supercontinent of Pangaea Ultima.

250 million years ago: Pangaea

A super ocean surrounds the supercontinent that scientists have named Pangaea. The first dinosaurs appeared on Pangaea.

150 million years ago

North America — • Europe Asia

South America — • Africa

For the last 200 million years, Pangaea has been slowly drifting apart. South America and Africa are slowly moving away from each other. The Atlantic Ocean is opening up between them.

65 million years ago

North America — • Europe Asia

Africa

South America — • India

Australia

By this time Pangaea has mostly broken up. Africa and India have split off. The dinosaurs became extinct quite suddenly around this time.

Present day

NorthAmerica Europe Asia

Africa • — India

South America

Australia

The map of the world that is familiar to us.

250 million years from now: Pangaea Ultima

Could this be what the world will look like in the distant future? Africa has collided with Europe, Australia with Asia. The Atlantic Ocean has disappeared. We can only imagine what forms of life might make their homes on this new supercontinent.

Plate tectonics

Why do the continents move? It is not really the continents that are moving. It is the **tectonic plates**. The continents get carried along like a child riding piggyback. The plates are massive slabs of material about 100 km (60 miles) thick. What could move such huge things?

Currents and continents

It is very hot at Earth's core—the temperature there is estimated to be 3,000 °C (5,400 °F) or more. This heat warms the bottom of the **mantle**, causing hot rock to rise up through Earth. Nearer the surface it cools and sinks back down again. This circular motion sets up powerful **convection currents** (movements in fluid) in the mantle.

The movement of rock in the mantle is incredibly slow. The hot rock rises up at a rate that is about 10,000 times slower than the hour hand on a clock. But this slow movement is strong enough to carry continents.

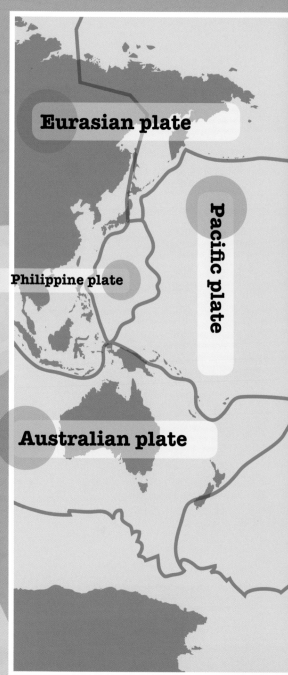

Eurasian plate

Pacific plate

Philippine plate

Australian plate

Map of the world's tectonic plates

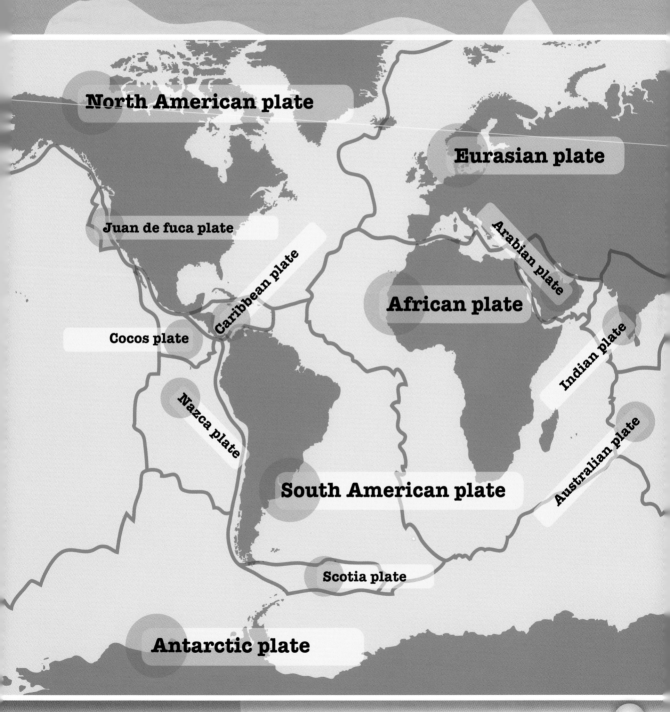

North American plate

Eurasian plate

Juan de fuca plate

Arabian plate

Caribbean plate

African plate

Cocos plate

Indian plate

Nazca plate

South American plate

Australian plate

Scotia plate

Antarctic plate

Moving Plates: Forming and Destroying

As the plates shift across Earth, they bump into each other, rub alongside each other, and move away from each other. This activity is powerful enough to create or destroy parts of Earth's **crust**.

Here two plates are moving apart from each other. **Magma** is rising up from the **mantle**. This forms new crust and fills the gap. These places are called constructive plate boundaries.

constructive plate boundary

magma

The growth of an ocean

Constructive plate boundaries are where new oceanic crust is formed. The process by which plates move apart to form new crust is called seafloor spreading. Over more than 100 million years, seafloor spreading has resulted in the Atlantic Ocean, for example. It has grown from a tiny inlet of water to a mighty ocean that separates continents.

Mid-Atlantic Ridge

As the Atlantic Ocean seafloor has spread, magma has risen to form the Mid-Atlantic Ridge. The ridge runs all the way down the middle of the ocean. It is a huge undersea mountain range that rises 300 m (980 ft) above the seafloor and is over 1,000 km (620 miles) wide.

The Mid-Atlantic Ridge is almost entirely beneath the Atlantic Ocean. Here it emerges as it runs through the country of Iceland.

WEGENER WAS RIGHT

When people first began to explore deep beneath the oceans, they made some amazing discoveries. The discovery of the Mid-Atlantic Ridge in the 1950s was important evidence. It led to an acceptance of Wegener's **theory** of continental drift. Along the ridge the ocean floor is spreading out at a rate of about 2.5 cm (1 in) per year. This might not seem much, but in 10 million years—not a lot of time in the history of Earth—it will have moved 250 km (155 miles).

Where plates collide

Earth isn't getting any bigger. If new crust is being created on the ocean floor, then the same amount of crust must be being destroyed somewhere else. This happens on Earth where oceanic and continental plates collide.

Destructive boundaries

Where plate boundaries come together, one plate may move beneath the other. These are called destructive plate boundaries because crust is destroyed here. The denser oceanic crust is forced into the **asthenosphere** below and melts away. This forms pockets of magma that rise toward the surface. As fast as new crust is forming ridges, it is being destroyed as it crashes into continents.

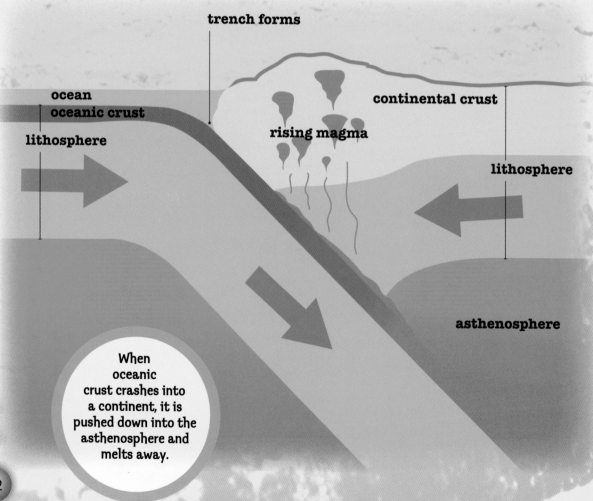

trench forms

ocean
oceanic crust

continental crust

lithosphere

rising magma

lithosphere

asthenosphere

When oceanic crust crashes into a continent, it is pushed down into the asthenosphere and melts away.

Trenches

Where the oceanic crust dives down into Earth, deep trenches are formed.

Along the edges of the Pacific Ocean there are a number of long, narrow trenches. They are thousands of kilometers in length. At the bottom of these trenches, the deepest parts of the ocean are found, 10 km (6 miles) beneath the surface.

Trenches in Earth's oceans can be explored using a diving bell. Diving bells carry people deep under water.

THE MARIANA TRENCH

Trenches are also found where two oceanic plates collide. In the Western Pacific is the Mariana Trench, the deepest place on Earth. It shows where the Pacific plate meets the Philippine plate, another ocean plate. At the southern end of the Mariana Trench is "Challenger Deep." It is so deep that the world's tallest mountain, Mount Everest, would disappear if it were dropped into it. The top would be more than 2,000 m (6,560 ft) beneath the ocean.

In 1960, the only ever manned exploration of "Challenger Deep" took place. Divers made the perilous journey beneath the waves using a specially-built craft called "Trieste."

Mountain building

When two continental plates collide, one doesn't just disappear beneath the other. The continents are not dense enough to be forced downward. Instead the crust is slowly pushed sideways or buckles (**folds**) up to form a mountain range. At destructive boundaries, too, mountains are formed as one plate pushes another upward as it slides beneath it. This is how the Rocky Mountains of North America were formed.

The Rocky Mountains of North America were formed over 120 million years ago. This happened when the Pacific plate collided with the North American plate.

TRY THIS — MAKE A MOUNTAIN RANGE

Roll out several rectangular sheets of modeling clay, each a different color. Lay them on top of one another. Now slowly push the ends of the clay sheets together using wooden blocks (you may find it easier to get a friend to push from one side while you push from the other). Watch how your "rock" layers buckle and fold to form a mountain range.

The Himalayas

The Himalayas form the highest mountain range in the world. They were created when India collided with the Eurasian plate around 50 million years ago. The plates crumpled up and over each other, pushing up the mountain range.

This massive collision still carries on today. Mount Everest , the highest peak in the Himalayas, is being pushed up about a centimeter a year. **Erosion** is wearing it away nearly as fast. It is also being moved about 3 cm (1 in) northeast each year as India continues slowly pushing into Asia.

India has been pushing northward into the Eurasian plate for millions of years. This collision has caused the land to crumple, forming the Himalayan mountain range.

Eurasian plate

India today

India 10 million years ago

Sri Lanka

India 38 million years ago

equator

India 55 million years ago

India 71 million years ago

Indian Ocean

FROM OCEAN FLOOR TO MOUNTAINTOP

The top of Mount Everest was once the bottom of the ocean that lay between India and Asia. **Fossils** of marine (sea-living) animals that are about 65 million years old have been found at the summit (top).

The Rock Cycle

Rocks in Earth's **crust** may seem to be permanent. But in fact they are constantly changing. They are transformed over time as they move through the **rock cycle**. The cycle is never-ending.

The life of rocks

Look at the diagram on the opposite page to see how rocks move through a cycle.

(1) New material is always being brought to the surface as **magma** rises up from below and escapes through volcanoes (see page 34). <u>**Magma that escapes to the surface is called lava**</u>. Rocks that form from cooling **lava** are called **igneous rocks**.

(2) Over long periods of time, the forces of **weathering** slowly break down the igneous rocks. Changes in temperature and the effects of rain and ice can eventually reduce the hardest rocks to fragments. The weathered fragments are carried away by wind and water. This is called **erosion**.

(3) Eventually layer upon layer of these rock fragments gather together. They often wash onto the seafloor as **sediment**. The layers above press the layers below so hard that they are compressed into rock again. This type of rock is called **sedimentary rock**.

(4) Plate movements shift the sedimentary rocks around. Some may be pushed up as plates collide to form mountains. This is called uplift. Some rocks may be pushed deeper into Earth.

(5) If the rocks go deep enough, they will melt. They can then be recycled as igneous rocks once more. Or they may be changed by temperature and pressure inside Earth. Rocks changed in this way are called **metamorphic rocks**. Each of the three types of rock may eventually be changed into one of the other types.

SHRINKING EARTH?

Long ago people struggled to explain how features such as mountains were formed. One popular idea in the 19th century was that Earth was shrinking and that mountains formed as the crust wrinkled up, like the skin on an old apple.

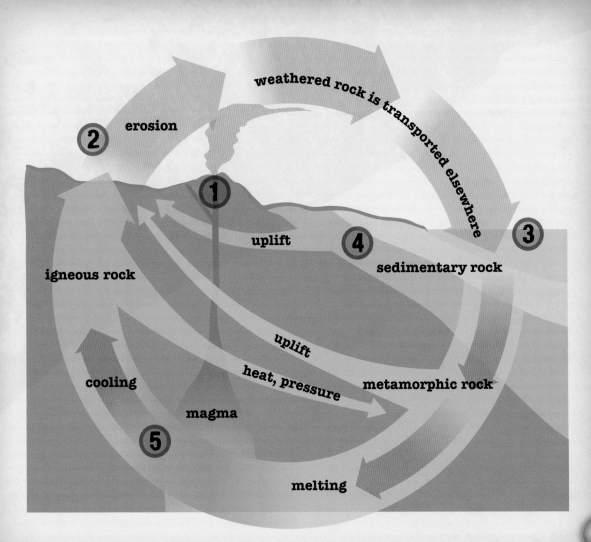

2 erosion

weathered rock is transported elsewhere

1

uplift

4

3

igneous rock

sedimentary rock

uplift

heat, pressure

cooling

metamorphic rock

magma

5

melting

EARTHQUAKES

Plates don't just move apart or crash into each other. They can move alongside each other, too. Most of these slipping and sliding plate boundaries are found on the ocean floor, but some are found on land. **Earthquakes occur where plates try to move past each other**.

Earthquakes

As plates move past each other, they don't slide by smoothly. They can get stuck together. Although the edges may be stuck, the rest of the plate keeps moving, building up energy. Eventually, the stuck edges suddenly break free and jolt forward again. Think of bending a stick. If you bend it enough, it will suddenly snap. This is what happens to the rocks when they can no longer resist the force of the moving plates. As they break, the energy built up is released as an earthquake that shakes the ground, sometimes violently. These breaks in the rocks are called **faults**.

plate 2
epicenter
plate 1
focus
shock waves

Shock waves

The sudden release of energy sends **shock waves** through Earth. The waves travel right around the planet. <u>**The exact point where an earthquake takes place is called the focus**</u>. This is usually deep under the ground. The point on the surface directly above this is called the epicenter (see page 28). This is where the shock waves are felt most strongly.

Earthquakes can be followed by a series of smaller shocks, called aftershocks. These are caused as the rocks settle in to their new position. Some shock waves make the ground ripple up and down, like waves on the water.

This computer simulation shows what a tsunami looks like as it crashes into a coastal city. There are no defenses against such a disaster.

On December 26, 2004, a massive tsunami caused great destruction. It took thousands of lives in countries around the Indian Ocean.

TSUNAMI

If an earthquake happens beneath the sea, it can trigger a massive tsunami. This is a giant wave of water that speeds across the ocean at 1,000 kph (620 mph). When the wave hits the coast, the damage can be devastating.

The 1,100-km (680-mile) long San Andreas Fault runs through California. Here the Pacific plate moves slowly past the North American plate. As the people who live here are all too aware, the result of this movement can be earthquakes.

Moving to Los Angeles

The rate of movement along the San Andreas Fault is around 5–6 cm (2 in) a year. Scientists predict that if this movement continues, San Francisco and Los Angeles will be next to each other in around 15 million years from now.

San Francisco 1906

In 1906 a powerful earthquake hit the city of San Francisco. Seven hundred people were killed and huge areas of the city were devastated. Fires that took three days to bring under control caused further damage. San Francisco was rebuilt and, within ten years, most traces of earthquake damage were gone.

Loma Prieta

The Loma Prieta earthquake of 1989 caused billions of dollars worth of damage. It killed around 60 people in the San Francisco Bay Area. Most lives were lost when part of the Interstate 880 collapsed.

Future quakes

The plates aren't going to stop moving, so further earthquakes along the San Andreas Fault will take place. In 1857 one of the strongest earthquakes ever struck southern California, hundreds of kilometers away from San Francisco. No one can predict just where, when, or how devastating the next one might be. Despite this, cities like San Francisco continue to grow and prosper.

Life on the margins

San Francisco is not the only major city to have been built in an earthquake zone. Tokyo, in Japan, and Mexico City, in Mexico, are at risk from earthquakes, too. Around 40 of the world's 50 fastest-growing cities are in earthquake zones.

THE KOBE DISASTER

1995

When an earthquake hit the city of Kobe in Japan in January 1995, it caused great damage. Around 5,000 people were killed and hundreds of thousands were left homeless. Many older, wooden houses collapsed. Office blocks built of steel and concrete collapsed in the middle. Modern buildings, designed to be earthquake proof, suffered little damage, although some were left standing at an angle.

The Japanese worked hard to fix the city after the earthquake. By July 1995, water, electricity, and gas had been restored. By August the railways were back in service. Today you would never know Kobe had been struck.

NOW

Rescue workers from Austria search for victims of the Bam earthquake in Iran. Specially-trained dogs help find people hidden beneath the rubble.

Economics and earthquakes

Preparation and response to earthquake disasters is better in some countries than others. Countries that are developed (advanced in technology) and wealthy, such as the United States and Japan, cope quite well. Poorer countries do not.

When a powerful earthquake struck the city of Bam in Iran in December 2003, over 43,000 people were killed. Poorly-built housing was blamed for many deaths. The mud-brick buildings simply collapsed. A similar-sized earthquake a few days earlier in California killed just three people, thanks largely to safer buildings.

There are over 500 active volcanoes on Earth. **Active volcanoes are mainly found along plate margins**. This is where the energy of plate movements is greatest. It generates enough heat in Earth's **mantle** to melt rock into **magma**. This magma is how an erupting volcano begins.

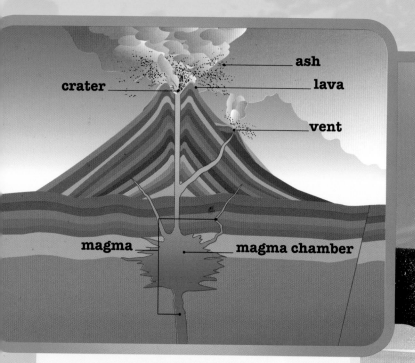

crater — ash — lava — vent — magma — magma chamber

In some places, the magma heats water beneath the ground so that it erupts in spectacular geysers.

Lava flows

In a volcanic eruption, molten rock and boiling hot gases move upward and break through weaknesses in the **crust**. They will erupt out in a **lava** flow. If the gas pressure is high enough, it will erupt out in a spectacular explosion, sending rocks and clouds of ash flying into the air.

The Ring of Fire

The Ring of Fire is an area around the Pacific Ocean that is dotted with volcanoes. More than half of the world's active volcanoes are found on the Ring of Fire. Most of the world's earthquakes happen here, too. Movements around the Pacific plate cause most of this activity.

volcanoes

San Andreas Fault

plate boundaries

Ring of Fire

Mid-Atlantic Ridge

Hot spots

Some volcanoes are located far from the plate edges. So how did they form? Scientists believe that in some places on Earth's mantle there are high-temperature hot spots under the plates. As an ocean plate moves slowly over the hot spot, it melts. Magma can then erupt through the crust forming an undersea volcano. This may eventually grow to become a volcanic island, like the islands of Hawaii.

Cinder cones, shields, lava domes, and stratovolcanoes

Not all volcanoes are the same. There are four main kinds: **cinder cones**, shields, lava domes, and stratovolcanoes.

Cinder cones Cinder cones are among the most common types of volcano. These are steep-sided hills built from **lava** fragments that build up around the vent (opening) of the volcano. Most have a bowl-shaped crater with a single vent. They can be anything from a few meters to several hundred meters high. A cinder cone can be formed from just a single eruption.

Shield volcanoes Shield volcanoes are massive. They are built up from several layers of lava that pour from one or more vents. They are broad and have gentle slopes. Shield volcanoes don't erupt explosively. The volcanoes of Hawaii, including Mauna Loa, are a chain of shield volcanoes.

Lava domes
Lava domes are formed by lava that doesn't flow well and forms a cap over a volcano's vent. The dome grows as it expands from within. It can reach hundreds of meters across. It may erupt catastrophically as pressure builds inside the volcano and becomes strong enough to blow the cap off.

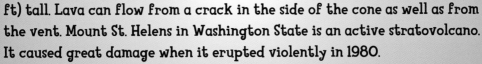

Stratovolcanoes
Stratovolcanoes are also known as composite volcanoes because they are formed from layers of different materials. Ash, cinders, and rocks shot from the vents, as well as cooled and hardened lava, all make up a stratovolcano. They can be as much as 2,500 m (8,200 ft) tall. Lava can flow from a crack in the side of the cone as well as from the vent. Mount St. Helens in Washington State is an active stratovolcano. It caused great damage when it erupted violently in 1980.

Calderas
A caldera is not a type of volcano. They are formed when the ground collapses as a result of a massive eruption. A caldera may be bigger than the biggest shield volcano. One such massive caldera in Yellowstone National Park was formed by an eruption that must have been thousands of times bigger than anything seen since. Calderas can be classed as supervolcanoes. Such eruptions are capable of covering an entire continent with ash.

Living with volcanoes

Why would people choose to live close to a volcano, knowing that it might erupt, putting their lives and property in danger?

Volcanic wealth

One reason that communities have grown near volcanoes is that volcanic soils are some of the most fertile in the world. This makes them ideal for farming. Volcanic lava often contains valuable **minerals**, such as gold, zinc, and copper. They make the area near a volcano appealing to settlers.

The coffee plantations in the Central American country of Guatemala grow well. The volcanic soil is very fertile and produces a high-quality coffee.

Unknown dangers

It is also possible that the people settling near a volcano could be unaware of the dangers. A volcano can stay dormant (asleep) for hundreds, if not thousands, of years. This gives plenty of time for towns and cities to become established in between eruptions.

Mount Pinatubo

In June 1991, Mount Pinatubo, a volcano in the north of the Philippines, erupted. It had been dormant for 600 years. A series of earthquakes gave warning that the volcano was reawakening. Many people were evacuated (moved away). Even so, more than 700 people were killed and nearly a quarter of a million buildings were destroyed. Avalanches of hot gas, ash, and rock poured from the volcano. Within hours of the eruption, rainwater from a tropical storm mixed with the ash on the sides of the volcano. This created a mudflow that raced down the slopes and caused further devastation around the volcano.

Eyes on the World

A lot of what we know about tectonic plates comes from Earth-orbiting satellite observations. Using Global Positioning System (GPS) technology, scientists can measure the speed and direction of plate movement. GPS surveys the land based on signals it receives from **satellites** in space.

Volcano monitoring

Other satellite systems use infrared detectors. Infrared is a wave of energy that is emitted (released) by heated objects. It is invisible to the human eye. By detecting the infrared, we can locate undersea volcanoes. Hot spots can be detected on volcanoes, too. This could indicate that **magma** is rising and an eruption is about to take place.

This photograph of an erupting volcano in Venezuela was taken from a satellite in orbit. The deep purple shows where **lava** has flowed through the surrounding forests.

Fast and slow

The world's plates aren't all moving at the same speed. The northern end of the Mid-Atlantic Ridge has the slowest rate, moving less than 2.5 cm (1 in) in a year. The East Pacific Rise, in the South Pacific, zips along at a speedy 15 cm (6 in) a year.

Earthquake warning?

Satellite imaging technology is so advanced that it can detect movements in the **crust** of just a millimeter. This kind of satellite observation may one day be able to give advance warnings of earthquakes.

A new sea

In the deserts of northern Ethiopia, a new sea is forming. There is no water there yet. But, the Arabian and African tectonic plates are slowly pulling apart. Millions of years from now, water will rush in to fill the gap. This is the same process that formed the Atlantic Ocean. Scientists have

tear in crust

sea will fill the gap

been able to study it in detail thanks to satellite observations. The satellite image above shows that a huge tear has opened up in Earth's crust. It is the biggest tear seen since satellite monitoring began.

Measuring earthquakes

There are different ways of recording the strength of earthquakes. The one you'll hear about most often in the news is the **Richter Scale**. This is based on **seismometer** (an instrument for detecting crust movements) readings. Scientists don't use this one any more as they don't consider it to be very accurate, especially when it comes to really big quakes. They prefer to use something called the **Moment Magnitude Scale**. The Moment Magnitude Scale is based on the amount of energy released by an earthquake and the size of the area affected by it. A third scale, the **Mercalli Scale**, describes earthquakes according to their effects.

The Richter Scale

The Richter Scale measures the intensity (force) of an earthquake. Each whole number the scale goes up represents a tenfold increase in the earthquake's intensity. In other words an earthquake rated 6.4 is ten times more powerful than one rated 5.4.

Less than 3.5 *Generally not felt by people but recorded on a seismometer.*

3.5–5.4 *Often felt by people but rarely causes much damage.*

Under 6.0 *May cause major damage to poorly constructed buildings. It is likely only to cause slight damage to well-designed buildings.*

6.1–6.9 *Much damage caused to buildings. Houses may be moved on their foundations.*

7.0–7.9 *Major earthquake. Can cause serious damage over large areas. Buildings collapse, and bridges are twisted and fall.*

8 or greater *Total destruction over a wide area. Objects will be thrown into the air by the **shock waves**.*

The Mercalli Scale

The Mercalli Scale describes the effects of an earthquake. Unlike the Moment Magnitude and Richter scales, it doesn't involve taking measurements with seismometers or other instruments. It is simply based on what people see and experience during an earthquake.

I. *People do not feel any movement.*

II. *A few people might notice movement, especially on the upper floors of tall buildings.*

III. *Many people indoors feel movement. Hanging objects swing back and forth.*

IV. *Most people indoors feel movement. Windows and doors rattle. Parked cars may rock and people outside feel movement.*

V. *Almost everyone feels movement. Doors swing open, and dishes may fall and break. Trees might shake outside.*

VI. *Everyone feels movement. People have trouble walking. Pictures fall off walls and furniture may be moved.*

VII. *People have trouble standing. Drivers feel their cars shaking. Loose bricks fall from buildings. Serious damage is done to poorly-built buildings.*

VIII. *Drivers have trouble controlling their cars. Houses might shift on their foundations. Tall structures such as towers might twist and fall. Poorly-built buildings suffer severe damage. Tree branches break.*

IX. *Even well-built buildings suffer considerable damage. Houses move off their foundations. Some underground pipes are broken. Cracks appear in the ground.*

X. *Most buildings and their foundations are destroyed. Some bridges are destroyed.* **Dams** *are seriously damaged. The ground cracks over large areas.*

XI. *Most buildings collapse. Large cracks appear in the ground. Underground pipelines are destroyed, and railroad tracks are badly bent.*

XII. *Almost everything is destroyed. Objects are thrown into the air as waves travel through the ground.*

QUICK QUIZ

1 How old do scientists believe Earth to be?
a) 100,000 years b) 4.5 million years
c) 4,000 years d) 4.5 billion years

2 What is the oldest type of **crust**?
a) pie b) continental c) bread d) oceanic

3 Which **continents** did Alfred Wegener believe had once fit together?
a) Australia and Antarctica b) Africa and Asia
c) South America and Africa d) North America and Asia

4 What was the name of the supercontinent thought to have existed 250 million years ago?
a) Narnia b) Hyperborea c) Atlantis d) Pangaea

5 In what part of Earth is rock melted into **magma**?
a) crust b) core c) mantle d) atmosphere

6 How many of the world's fastest-growing cities have been built in earthquake zones?
a) 15 b) 10 c) 40 d) 100

7 How fast do the fastest-moving **tectonic plates** move?
a) 15 kph (9 mph) b) 1.5 m (5 ft) a day
c) 1.5 m (5 ft) a year d) 15 cm (6 in) a year

Answers on page 47

Glossary

caldera large circular basin created when a large explosion destroys a volcano, or a volcano collapses

cinder cone volcano largely formed of rock fragments rather than lava

continental crust part of Earth's crust that makes up the continents. On average it is about 30 km (20 miles) thick, but up to 70 km (45 miles) thick beneath mountain ranges.

continental shelf shallow underwater boundary between a continent and the deep ocean

continents seven large landmasses of Earth

convection currents movements within a fluid caused by hotter material rising above cooler material

core central part of Earth, beginning about 2,900 km (1,800 miles) beneath the surface

crust outer layer of Earth, divided into continental and oceanic crust

currents movements in a liquid or gas

dam strong barrier built across a river to hold back the water

earthquake shaking of the ground caused by the sudden movement of rocks in the crust

erosion process of being worn away by wind or water

eruption sudden forcing of lava out through a volcano

fault fracture in Earth's crust along which rocks have moved. Most faults occur in groups called fault zones near plate boundaries.

fold buckling of rocks in the crust caused by compression as plates collide

fossil remains of a plant or animal that has been buried beneath the ground and has turned to rock over millions of years

igneous rock rock that was once molten and has become solid again

landmass vast body of land

lava magma that has reached the surface of Earth

magma molten rock found beneath Earth's surface. Magma that reaches the surface, through volcanoes for example, is called lava.

mantle part of Earth that lies between the crust and the core, roughly 30 to 2,900 km (20 to 1,800 miles) beneath the surface

margin boundary edge

Mercalli Scale scale for measuring earthquakes based on the effects felt by humans and their surroundings

metamorphic rock rock that has been changed by high pressures and temperatures inside Earth without actually melting

meteorites pieces of rock that fall to Earth from outer space

minerals substances found in nature. Rocks are made from a lot of minerals.

molten melted, in a liquid form

Moment Magnitude Scale scale that measures earthquakes based on the size of area affected

naturalists experts in the study of animals or plants

oceanic crust part of Earth's crust that lies beneath the ocean floor. From 6 to 10 km (4 to 6 miles) thick, it is largely made of basalt rock.

Richter Scale scale used for measuring the intensity of an earthquake

rock cycle unending cycle of rock formation and destruction

satellite any object, natural or artificial, that orbits another object in space. The international space station and the Moon are both satellites of Earth.

sediment pieces of rock that have been worn away and moved to another place

sedimentary rock rock that is formed from layers of the remains of older rocks that have been squeezed together

seismometer device used to detect shock waves traveling through Earth caused by earthquakes

shield area of ancient rock at the heart of a continent

shield volcano low, gently-sloping volcano formed from lava that has solidified

shock waves waves of energy sent out when, for example, rocks are shifted beneath Earth by an earthquake

tectonic plates 20 or so continental and oceanic plates that make up Earth's crust. The movements of the plates are responsible for earthquakes and volcanoes and for the changing positions of the continents over millions of years.

theory best explanation that can be found for why something happens based on careful observation and experiment

tsunami fast-moving wave generated by an earthquake taking place under the ocean

weathering breakdown of rock on or near Earth's surface

Find Out More

Books

Fradin, Judy and Dennis. *Witness to Disaster: Earthquakes.* Des Moines, IA: National Geographic Children's Books, 2008.

Johnson, Rebecca L. *Plate Tectonics.* New York: Lerner Publications, 2005.

Prager, Ellen J. *Jump Into Science: Earthquakes.* Des Moines, IA: National Geographic Children's Books, 2007.

Silver, Donald M. and Wynne, Patricia J. *The Amazing Earth Model Book.* New York: Scholastic, 1999.

Van Rose, Susanna. *Volcanoes and Earthquakes.* New York: DK Children, 2008.

Websites

http://www.ucmp.berkeley.edu/geology/tectonics.html
Plate tectonics—animated: A detailed guide to the history and science of plate tectonics, including animations of moving continents; from the University of California Museum of Paleontology in Berkeley.

http://www.cotf.edu/ete/modules/msese/earthsysflr/plates1.html
Plate tectonics: An easy to read introduction to plate tectonics and plate boundaries, from the Center for Educational Technologies.

http://tsunami.geo.ed.ac.uk/local-bin/quakes/mapscript/home.pl
The World-wide Earthquake Locator: Find out where earthquakes have taken place around the world—and where they might happen next, on this site from the University of Edinburgh's Earth Observatory.

http://earthquake.usgs.gov/learning/kids/
Earthquakes for Kids: Everything you would want to know about earthquakes, including cool facts, animations, and pictures, from the U.S. Geological Survey.

http://www.learner.org/interactives/volcanoes/
Volcanoes—can we predict volcanic eruptions?: An interactive guide to what goes on inside a volcano and what happens when one erupts.

http://earthobservatory.nasa.gov/Features/Wegener/
Alfred Wegener: An introduction to the life and work of Alfred Wegener, whose theory of continental drift transformed our understanding of Earth.

Quick Quiz Answers

1. d, **2.** b, **3.** c, **4.** d, **5.** c, **6.** c, **7.** d

Index